Hear the Wind Blow

written by **doe boyle**   illustrated by **emily paik**

ALBERT WHITMAN & COMPANY
Chicago, Illinois

Awaken to the calm—

the peaceful pink of dawn's light,

quiet as the inky night.

Note a kiss of air—

a soft breath, a phantom wisp,

faint as shadows, cool and crisp.

Bend an ear to the breeze—

hear the scuffling, ruffling flutter—

leaves go scuttling in the gutter.

See the shifting grasses shudder—

sharing whispered summer secrets

with the silent, stalking egrets.

Watch the smoke of campfires rise—

tendrils drift toward clouded skies.

Flames that lick, sparks that flicker;

now the breeze grows bolder, quicker.

Listen to the riffling tide—

shorebirds soar and seagulls glide.

Crested wavelets toss the ocean;

wind creates their restless motion.

Hist wist, tilt an ear—

    hear the willows sway and scurry.

    Wind comes rushing,

    in a hurry.

Push against its mighty blast—

dash through raindrops!

Quick! Be fast!

Feel the twigs snap as you skitter—

branches break, leaves make litter.

Hasten now! Run for shelter—

the gale is coming, helter-skelter.

Now the windstorm whips and wails—

sucks at sand and billows sails.

Shut the doors! Stay inside.

A storm approaches! You must hide.

Meddling wind tugs battened hatches,

drums at windows, pulls at latches.

Sing out loud while gusts come tumbling.

You can match their roar and rumbling.

Now the storm is fierce and wild—

    you are safe, though, dauntless child.

    Nested, cozy, quilts piled round,

    you drown out the fearsome sound.

When the hurricane comes roiling,

    popcorn's popped, the kettle's boiling.

    While the tumult makes its din,

    you and yours are snug within.

    Swells with crashing crests and troughs

    spew white sea-foam far aloft.

    Salty spray pelts sodden beaches;

    thrashing air screams and screeches.

    Dories swamp; the thunder's clapping;

    schooners rock, their rigging slapping.

    Wires droop, and tree roots shudder—

    the world's atilt, without a rudder.

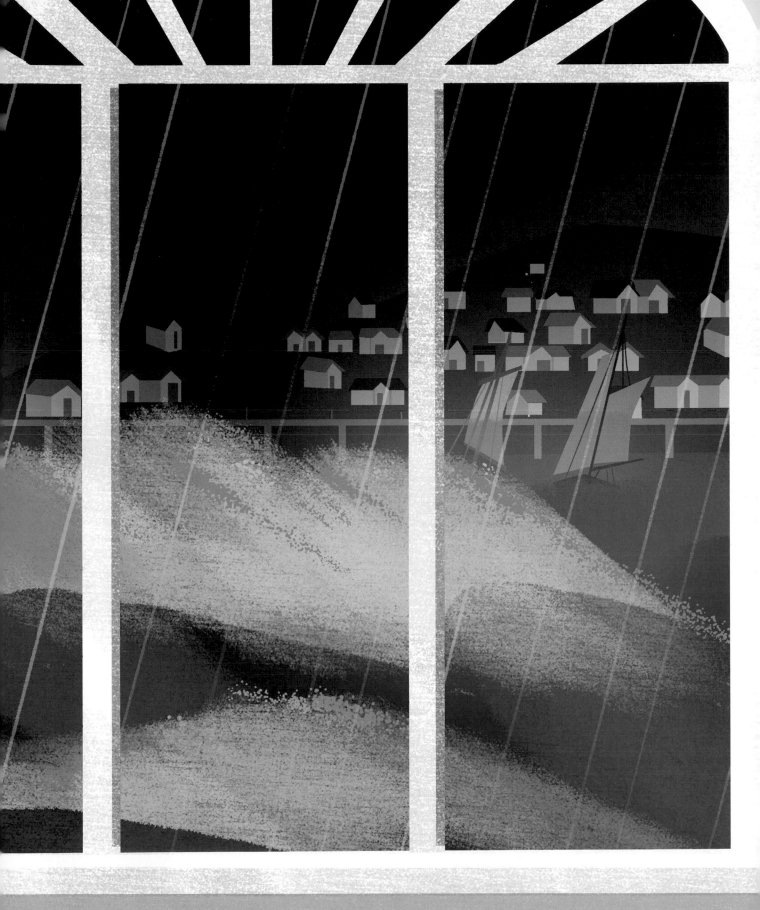

Hours later, winds calm down.

Stillness echoes through the town.

Lanes and streets lie pooled and puddled.

Flags are spent, and gardens muddled,

Flowers sag, and yards are flooded;

watch your step or you'll get mudded.

Friends and neighbors mop up floors;

they wring out rags and come outdoors.

Some share stories; some need help.

Beach folk rake the stranded kelp.

All the windswept world spins on.

Worry not! The storm is gone.

Yet you must listen! Heed each sound,

as the Earth turns round and round.

The wind moves on—it rarely tarries—

but on its currents, your voice carries.

Author's Note

This poem describes some of the many ways that wind affects our world. Each stanza represents, in order, one of the thirteen categories of the Beaufort wind force scale, from 0 to 12. The Beaufort scale, used by sailors and other people all around the world, is a description of the speed of the wind. It is based on the ways that human beings can feel and see the effects that the wind has on the sea, on the land, and even on people. But what exactly *is* wind?

Wind is air in motion.

Warm air weighs less than cold air. When air is warm, it rises. As the warm air rises above land or water, heavier cool air rushes into the open space left behind. That movement of air is wind. The faster the air moves, the stronger the wind will be.

Winds can be warm and blow softly, or they can be cool, making us comfortable on hot days. Winds can also be dangerous. They can be icy cold, carrying snow and sleet. Winds can whip the sea and bring slashing rain, as hurricanes do when they form over a warm ocean.

The Beaufort Wind Force Scale

The Beaufort wind force scale is a chart that helps us understand the speed and strength of the wind. Organized in numbered categories based on how fast wind is traveling, the scale tells us how the moving air changes conditions on land and on the sea. It tells us what we might see when the air is still, and it shows what we might see when a wind begins to blow faster and faster, harder and harder. Sailors can decide if the sea is safe for sailing; farmers can decide whether it is a good day to sow seeds or harvest a crop. You can use the Beaufort scale to help you decide if it is a good day to fly a kite, go for a hike, or swim in the sea.

The Beaufort scale is both useful and artful. It shows us each change in the wind in thirteen clear and separate categories, from 0 to 12—from calm air with little or no movement to powerful hurricanes with destructive force. Just like great poetry, the precise language of the Beaufort scale engages all the senses.

The scale that we use today is named for Admiral Sir Francis Beaufort, a British naval commander. He created a version of this scale around 1806. At that time, mariners did not have the special instruments we use today to measure the speed, or velocity, of the wind. Even though the explorer Ferdinand Magellan had already sailed around the world and Captain James Cook was already exploring the southern hemisphere, few people seemed to understand *why* the winds blew. A few scientists and writers had tried to organize their observations of the wind into a descriptive system, but none caught on until Beaufort borrowed from their scales and devised his own.

Still in use across the globe, the Beaufort scale now includes the wind's effects on land, buildings, and people. The modern scale also includes wind speed, in both miles per hour and in knots, which is measured by nautical instruments. The scale helps us to know when it is safe to sail and when it is wise to find shelter.

Number	Speed		Force
	knots	mph	
0	<1	<1	calm
1	1–3	1–3	light air
2	4–6	4–7	light breeze
3	7–10	8–12	gentle breeze
4	11–16	13–18	moderate breeze
5	17–21	19–24	fresh breeze
6	22–27	25–31	strong breeze
7	28–33	32–38	moderate gale (or near gale)
8	34–40	39–46	fresh gale (or gale)
9	41–47	47–54	strong gale
10	48–55	55–63	whole gale
11	56–63	64–72	storm
12	>64	>72	hurricane

Sea Effects	Land Effects
sea like mirror	smoke rises vertically; no perceptible movement
ripples with appearance of scales; no foam crests	smoke drifts slowly downwind, revealing wind direction; tree leaves barely move
wavelets, small but pronounced; crests of glassy appearance, not breaking	wind can be felt on face; leaves rustle; small twigs move; weather vanes move
large wavelets; crests begin to break; scattered whitecaps or "white horses"	leaves and twigs in constant motion; dry leaves blow up from ground; hair and clothing disturbed; light flags extend
small waves, becoming longer; numerous whitecaps/white horses	small branches on trees move; wind raises dust and loose paper and drives them along; hair disarranged
moderate waves, taking longer form; many whitecaps/white horses; some spray; crested wavelets form on inland water	large branches and small trees in leaf begin to sway; disagreeable wind force felt on body
larger waves forming; whitecaps everywhere; extensive white-foam crests; more spray	large branches sway in continuous motion; difficult to walk steadily; umbrellas hard to control; wires whistle
sea heaps up; white foam from breaking waves begins to be blown in streaks	whole trees in motion; inconvenience in walking
moderately high waves of greater length; edges of crests begin to break into sea spray; foam is blown in well-marked streaks	twigs and small branches break off trees; progress in walking is impeded; difficult to walk
high waves; wave crests topple and tumble, and sea begins to roll; dense streaks of foam; spray may reduce visibility	large branches break off trees; ground littered with broken branches; slight structural damage to chimney pots and bricks and to roofing tiles and slates; people blown over by wind force
very high waves with overhanging crests; sea takes white appearance as foam is blown in very dense streaks; rolling of sea is heavy and shock-like, and visibility is poor	trees broken or uprooted; minor to considerable structural damage
exceptionally high waves, sometimes concealing small and medium-sized ships; sea completely covered with long, white patches of foam; edges and crests have froth; visibility further reduced	widespread damage
air filled with foam; sea completely white with driving spray; visibility greatly reduced	violent movement of trees and severe and extensive destruction

Glossary

gale: a very brisk current of wind that moves more rapidly than a stiff breeze but slower than a hurricane. The Beaufort scale has four strengths of gale, from fresh gale to whole gale. Gales range from 32 to 63 mph, or 28 to 55 kn.

hurricane: a severe storm, characterized by extreme fury, sudden changes of the wind, and heavy rain, thunder, and lightning. Hurricanes occur most often in the Caribbean Sea, the Gulf of Mexico, the North Atlantic Ocean, and in the China Sea (where they are known as typhoons). Hurricane winds move at speeds greater than 74 mph, or 64 kn; on the Beaufort scale, they are a 12.

miles per hour (mph): a measurement of speed that expresses the number of miles that can be traveled in one hour. One mile per hour is equal to 1.4667 feet per second, or approximately 0.8689 kn.

knots (kn): A knot (pronounced "not") is a measurement of speed used for sea travel; one knot is the speed required to travel one nautical mile in one hour.

weather vane: a movable device, usually attached to a roof, steeple, or spire, that shows the direction of the wind.

Suggested Reading for Children

Asch, Frank, and Devin Asch. *Like A Windy Day*. New York: Houghton Mifflin Harcourt, 2008.

Bauer, Marion Dane. *Wind*, Ready-to-Read Level 1. New York: Simon Spotlight, 2003.

Cobb, Vicki. *I Face the Wind*, Science Play. New York: HarperCollins, 2003.

Dorros, Arthur. *Feel the Wind*, Let's-Read-and-Find-Out Science Level 2. New York: HarperCollins, 1990.

Malone, Peter. *Close to the Wind: The Beaufort Scale*. New York: G. P. Putnam, 2007.

Sherman, Josepha. *Gust and Gales: A Book about Wind*. Minneapolis, MN: Picture Window, 2004.

With loving gratitude to Judy Theise and in
loving memory of Jerry Theise. Under their roof,
I listen to the wind each summer.—DB

For my dear friend Doori—EP

Library of Congress Cataloging-in-Publication data is on file with the publisher.

Text copyright © 2021 Doe Boyle

Illustrations copyright © 2021 by Albert Whitman & Company

Illustrations by Emily Paik

First published in the United States of America in 2021 by Albert Whitman & Company

ISBN 978-0-8075-4561-4 (hardcover)

ISBN 978-0-8075-4562-1 (ebook)

Printed in China

10 9 8 7 6 5 4 3 2 1 RRD 24 23 22 21 20

Design by Aphelandra

For more information about Albert Whitman & Company,
visit our website at www.albertwhitman.com.